What We Wear

Diane James & Sara Lynn

Illustrated by Joe Wright

TWO-CAN

Work & Play

We need to wear clothes to protect our bodies. We wear warm clothes in winter and cool clothes in summer. Different fabrics suit different climates. People who do dangerous jobs often wear protective clothing, such as helmets and gloves. All over the world, people love dressing up in brightly coloured costumes to celebrate special occasions. We are going to look at where different fabrics come from and at some of the clothes people wear for work and play.

Warm & Woolly

One of the warmest, softest fabrics comes from sheep. Once a year sheep are brought in for clipping. A sheep shearer holds the sheep gently between his legs and clips the woolly coat off. An expert can clip about 250 sheep in one day!

When the wool has been washed it is very tangled. The clean wool is passed through rollers covered in tiny wire teeth which help to untangle it.

Then the wool goes to machines which twist and spin it into long lengths of yarn. Later, it is knitted or woven into fabric.

The wool that comes off the sheep's back is very dirty. It has to be washed thoroughly with soap and hot water. Then it is rinsed, squeezed through rollers and dried.

There are lots of different kinds of sheep. Some have long, shaggy coats and some short, curly coats. Because wool is a warm fabric it is used for winter clothes, such as sweaters, gloves, scarves and hats.

Pompons

Try making some of these jolly woolly pompons to decorate your winter clothes.

Get ready...
Cardboard
Wool (different colours)

2 Put one circle on top of the other. Wind some wool into a small ball and wrap it round and round the card circles. Keep going until the hole in the middle has almost disappeared. You could use different colours of wool.

Get set, go!

1 Cut two circles the same size from a piece of cardboard. You could use the ones here as a guide. Ask a grown-up to help you cut a small circle in the middle of each of them.

3 Ask a grown-up to help snip through the layers of wool at the edge.

4 Tie a length of wool round the middle of the pompon between the two pieces of card. Pull the card circles away from the pompon.

You could use your pompons to decorate a woolly hat, sweater or scarf.

Cool Cotton

Cotton is a cool, crisp fabric made from the cotton plant. It is light and soft and especially good for summer clothes.

Cotton plants grow best in sunny places. After the plant has flowered, seed pods form. When they ripen they look like fluffy, white cotton wool.

The cotton seed pods can be picked by machine or by hand. A different machine cleans and dries the pods and presses them into huge bundles. These are sent to a factory where they are spun into thread.

The cotton thread on the reels above is used for sewing. Other cotton thread may be made into fabrics like the ones below. The fabric can then be made into clothes.

In hot countries, people often wear long, flowing cotton robes to protect them from the fierce heat.

Print It!

Get ready...
Cardboard
Thin sponge
Cotton T-shirt
Fabric paints
(make sure you read the instructions on the paints)

Get set, go!

1 Draw a simple pattern on a piece of paper and decide what colours to use.

2 Ask a grown-up to cut the sponge into the shapes to make up your pattern. Glue each piece of sponge to a piece of cardboard.

3 Use a brush to cover one of the sponge shapes with paint. Press the shape down on to the shirt. Lift the cardboard off.

4 Do the same thing with the other shapes, using different colours for each one.

Silk Spinning

Silk is beautifully soft and very strong. It is spun by silkworms – caterpillars of special moths.

Silkworms have huge appetites and feed on leaves from the mulberry tree. About six weeks after hatching, a silkworm spins a web. It spins for about three days making a cocoon around itself.

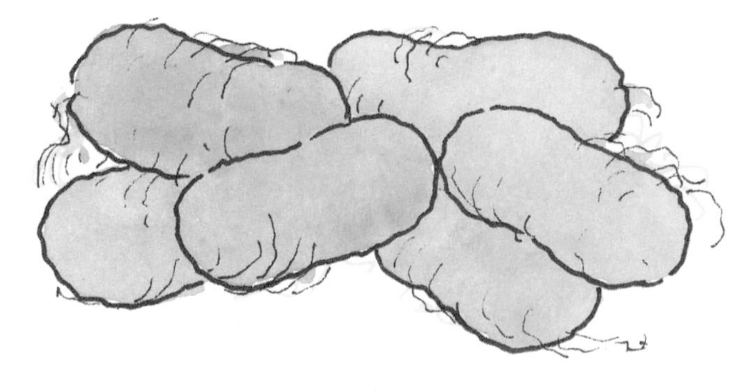

Silk workers unwind the threads of the cocoon. One cocoon can give about 1,000 metres of thread!

Silk is a good fabric to wear in hot countries because it is cool and light. This Indian lady is wearing clothes made from brightly coloured silk. She has wrapped a length round her head and shoulders.

Silk is often used to make clothes for special occasions. This young Chinese boy is wearing a silk robe embroidered with dragons. Just think how busy the silkworms must have been to spin enough thread to make this beautiful costume!

Fabrics

Wool, silk and cotton yarns can all be used to make fabrics. They are either woven or knitted into long lengths. The card weaving loom below shows how threads are woven in and out of each other to make a piece of fabric. Weaving can be done by hand or by machine. Huge machines can produce fabric very quickly – it is much slower by hand!

Coloured yarns can be woven into complicated patterns. The woman in the picture below is weaving a length of fabric. The leather strap keeps her loom in position. Look at the knitting on the needle here. You will see that knitted fabric is made up of a series of loops. Different colours have been used to make stripes. Knitting can also be done by hand or machine.

Knitted fabrics are more stretchy than woven ones. They are good for sweaters. The neck stretches to allow your head through and then goes back to its original shape! Knitted fabrics are also good for sports clothes because they allow you to move easily.

Paper Weaving

Here is a good way to see how weaving works by doing it yourself.

Get ready...
Coloured paper
Scissors

Get set, go!
1 Take a rectangle of paper and fold it in half. Cut slits at equal distances from the folded edge to within about 2 centimetres of the outside edge.

2 Unfold the rectangle.
3 Cut strips of coloured paper about 1 centimetre wide and as long as the width of the rectangle.
4 Starting at one end of the rectangle, weave a strip of paper over and under each slit. Take another strip of paper and weave this in and out above the first strip. Where the first strip goes under, the second strip should go over.

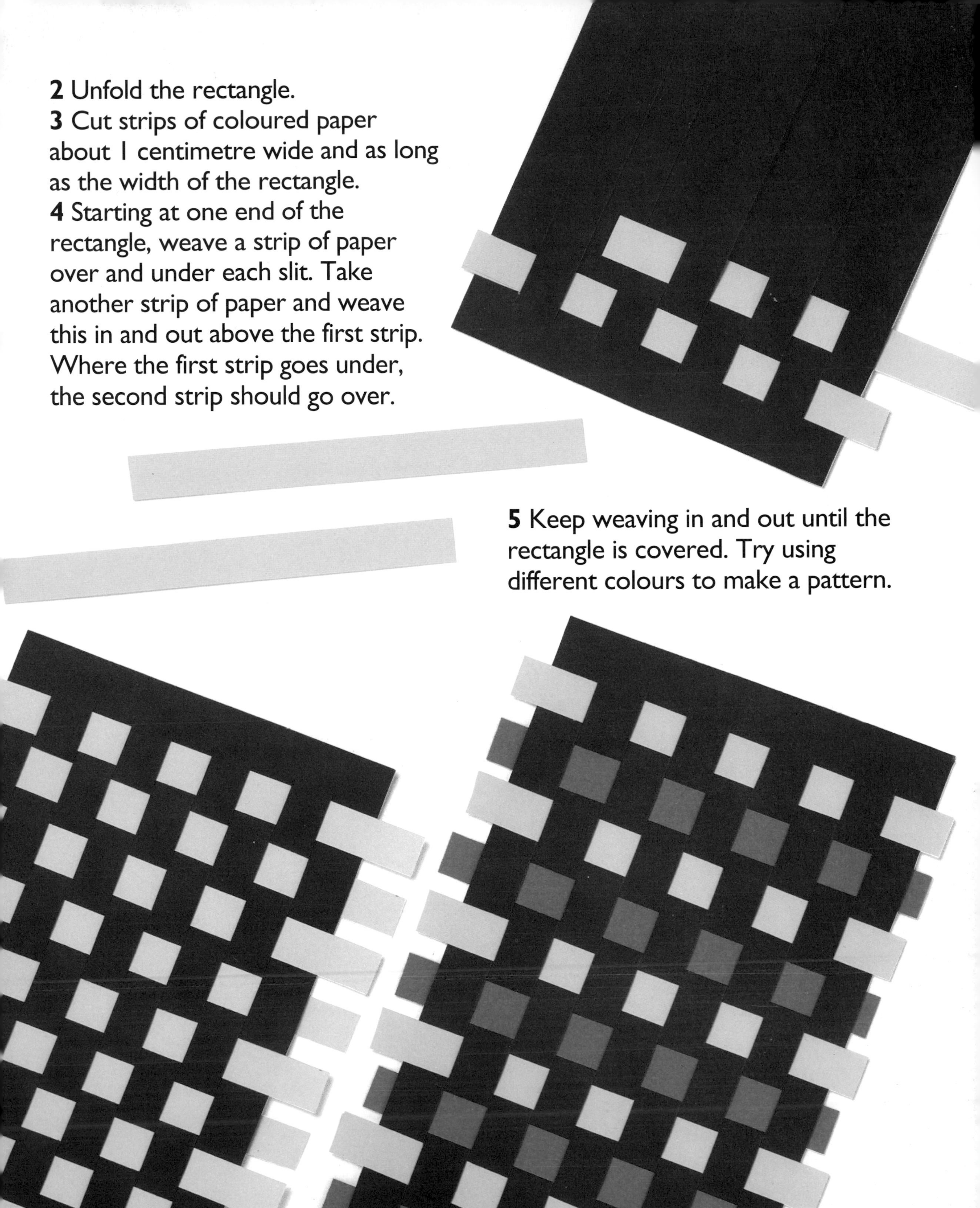

5 Keep weaving in and out until the rectangle is covered. Try using different colours to make a pattern.

Rubber

What do you wear when it is raining to keep you dry? Do you wear rubber boots and a rubber coat? Rubber is a very useful material. It is waterproof, stretchy, airtight and lasts for a long time.

When the bark of the rubber tree is cut, a white juice oozes out. It is caught in bowls strapped to the trunk. The juice is called latex and can be made into rubber.

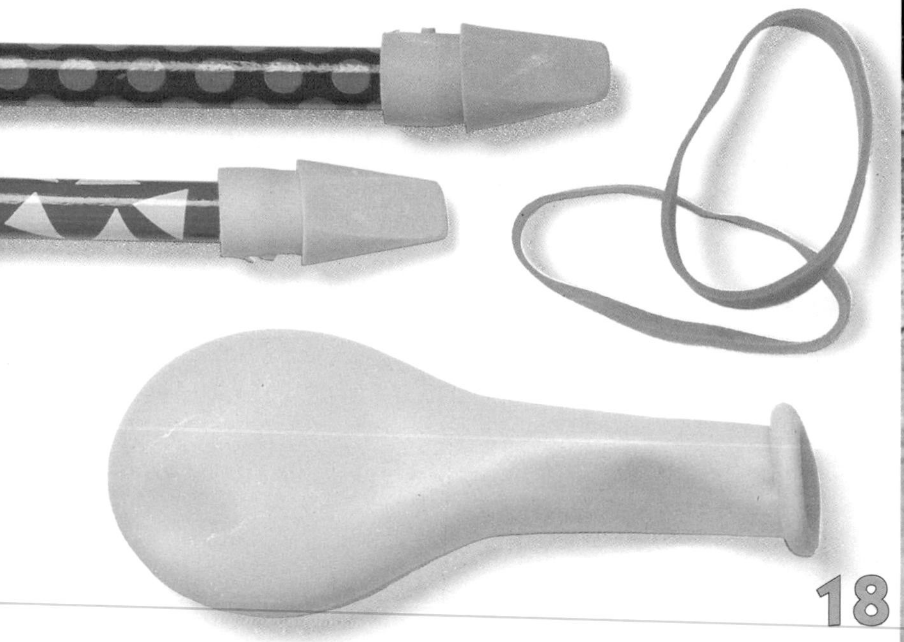

Hundreds of years ago, Indians in South America discovered a clever way to protect their feet.

They spread latex from rubber trees on their feet and let it dry. This made a type of rubber shoe!

Rubber is used to make elastic bands and balloons. Balls are often made from rubber. It makes them bounce!

Fun Clothes

Sometimes people dress up for special occasions. They may be actors taking part in a play, or dancers putting on a performance. They may be going to a wedding, or perhaps a party! Do you ever dress up?

In some countries, people have national costumes. These people are from Holland.

People spend days and days making colourful costumes to wear for festivals and carnivals. This amazing dragon is helping to celebrate Chinese New Year.

This beautiful head-dress and funny mask completely hide the dancer wearing them. If you would like to make your own mask, look at the next page!

Guess Who!

The next time you have a party, why not ask your friends to wear masks. You could give a prize for the best one! Here is one for you to make.

Get ready...
Coloured paper or thin card
Scissors
Glue
Cord or elastic

Get set, go!
1 Cut out an oval shape like the one on the page opposite. Ask a grown-up to help you cut two holes for your eyes.
2 Cut different shapes from coloured paper and glue them on to your mask.
3 Make a small hole at each side of the mask and poke some cord through. Tie the cord at the back of your head to keep the mask in place.

Dress It Up

Even the plainest clothes can be made to look exciting! You can wear brightly coloured jewellery, such as necklaces, and bracelets. Or, decorate your clothes with beads and shiny sequins. Hats, gloves and bags can also be used to brighten up an outfit. Look at the next page to get some ideas for making your own jewellery.

In Africa people spend hours and hours making their beautiful beaded head-dresses and necklaces. They must feel heavy to wear!

These girls from Thailand have beads and silver ornaments sewn on to their clothes. The flowers on their hats are made from lengths of brightly coloured wool.

Beads

Get ready...
Clay (look for the type that hardens in the air)
Macaroni
Flour
Salt
Water
Paint and paintbrush
Cord
Toothpick or knitting needle (for making holes through beads)

Get set, go!
Macaroni Beads
1 Paint dry macaroni pieces with bright colours.
2 Thread them on to coloured cord.

Get set, go!
Clay Beads
1 Roll a piece of clay into a long sausage shape.
2 Cut off small pieces and roll them into small balls to make beads.
3 Poke a hole through the middle of each bead.
4 Leave the beads to dry hard and paint them in bright colours.
5 Thread the beads on to a length of cord.

Get set, go!
Salt Dough Beads

1 Put 2 cups of flour, 1 cup of salt and 1 cup of water into a large mixing bowl. Mix the dough together until it forms a ball.

2 Put the ball on to a floured surface and knead it with your hands until it is smooth. Break off small pieces of dough and roll them between your palms to make beads.

3 Use a toothpick or knitting needle to make a hole.

4 Ask a grown-up to put the beads on a baking tray and bake them in the oven for about half an hour at a low temperature. When they are cold you can paint them and thread them on to a length of cord.

Cover Up

Sometimes we need clothes to protect us. For example, if someone is doing a dangerous job, like welding, they will wear a mask to protect their eyes from the bright light and heat.

Astronauts wear spacesuits which cover their heads and bodies completely. When they are on the moon's surface the suits allow them to breathe and move around easily. Their boots are weighted to stop the astronauts floating away!

Some sports can be dangerous! The ice hockey player in the photograph is wearing a mask and helmet to protect his face and head, and pads on his arms and legs. Horse riders wear special hats to protect their heads in case of a fall. Can you see what the skateboarder in the picture here is wearing?

Cooper
WINNWELL
Cooper
SHOK-GUARD

Quiz

1 Where do these people come from?

3 What sort of fabric do you think the clothes in this picture are made from?

2 What do you think these beads are made from?

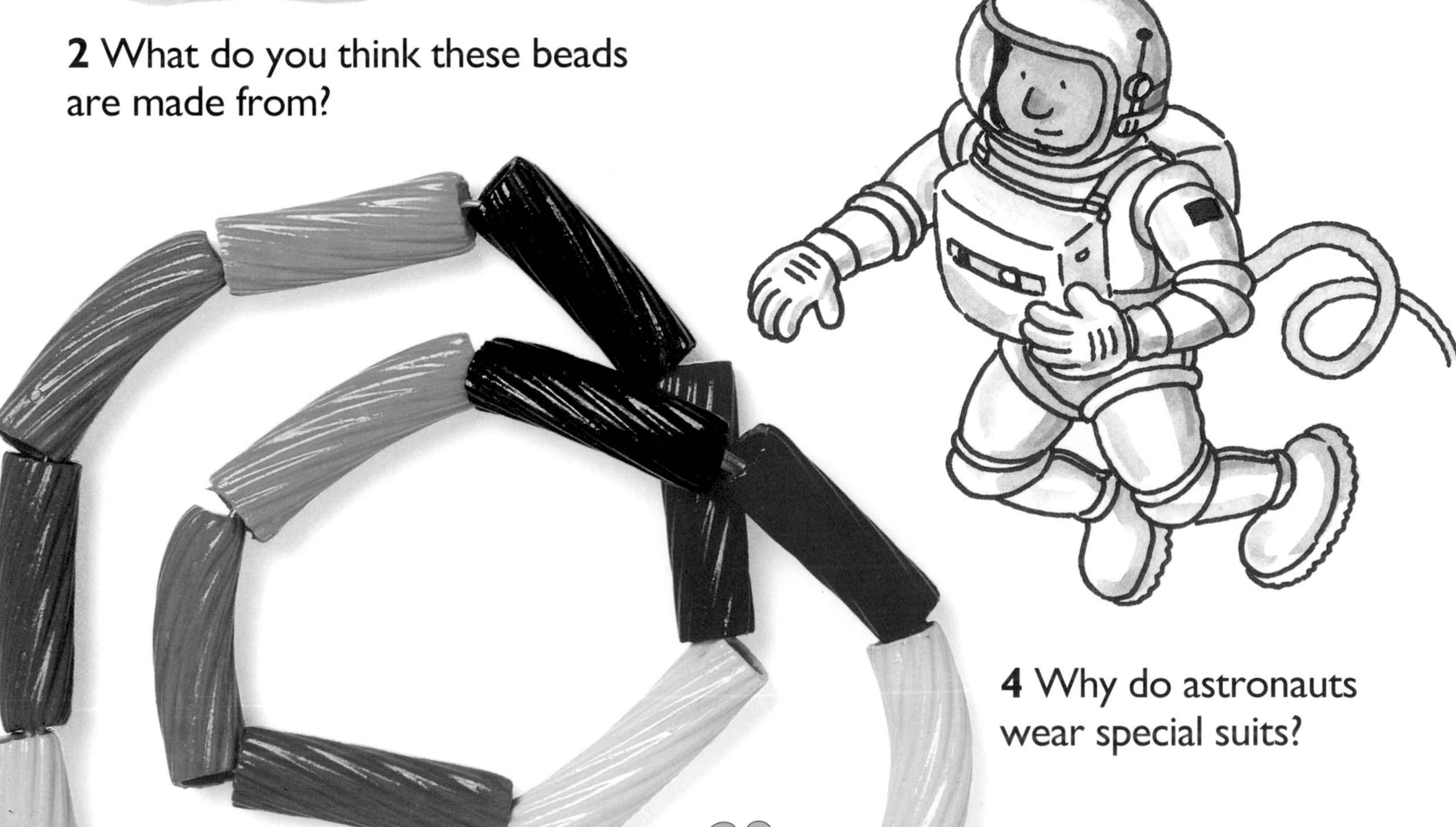

4 Why do astronauts wear special suits?

5 What do you think this man is doing?

6 What is this white juice made into?

7 Do you know what this is?

Index

Question Answers

p29
Q. Can you see what the woman in the picture is using to weave the threads with?
A. A loom.
p28
Q. Can you see what the skateboarder is wearing?
A. A helmet, knee-pads and elbow-pads.

p30-31
1 Holland.
2 Dry macaroni.
3 Cotton.
4 So that they can breathe and walk on the surface of the moon.
5 Shearing sheep.
6 Rubber.
7 Wool.

Photo credits Cover, p. 12, p. 24-25 Spectrum Colour Library; p. 2-3 Pictures Colour Library; p. 5, p. 9, p. 19 Tony Stone Worldwide; p. 4, p. 6-7, p. 8, p. 10-11, p. 12-13, p. 14-15, p. 16-17, p. 18, p. 22-23, p. 24-25 (background), p. 26-27 Steve Shott; p. 13, p. 21 Britstock–IFA; p. 28 Image Bank

First published in Great Britain in 1994 by
Two-Can Publishing Ltd., 346 Old Street,
London EC1V 9NQ
in association with Scholastic Publications Ltd.

Printed and bound in Hong Kong 2 4 6 8 10 9 7 5 3 1

A catalogue record for this book is available from the British Library

Pbk ISBN: 1-85434-229-0
Hbk ISBN: 1-85434-228-2